CONT

CW00780183

Poetry Book Society

CHOICE SELECTORS RECOMMENDATION SPECIAL COMMENDATION	SANDEEP PARMAR & ANDREW McMILLAN
TRANSLATION SELECTOR	GEORGE SZIRTES
PAMPHLET SELECTORS	A.B. JACKSON & DEGNA STONE
WILD CARD SELECTOR	ANTHONY ANAXAGOROU
CONTRIBUTORS	SOPHIE O'NEILL NATHANIEL SPAIN KATIE POUNDER BRIANNA ROSE
EDITORIAL & DESIGN	ALICE KATE MULLEN

Membership Options

Associate 4 *Bulletins* a year (UK £22, Europe £35, Rest of the World £42)
Full 4 Choice books and 4 *Bulletins* a year (£55, £65, £75)
Charter 20 books and 4 *Bulletins* (£180, £210, £235)
Education 4 books, 4 *Bulletins*, posters, teaching notes (£79, £89, £99)
Charter Education 20 books, 4 *Bulletins*, posters, teaching notes (£209, £245, £275)
Translation 4 Translation books and 4 *Bulletins* (£65, £90, £99)
Student 4 Choice books and 4 *Bulletins* (£35, £55, £65)
Translation Plus Full 4 Choices, 4 *Bulletins* & 4 Translation books (£98, £120, £132)
Translation Plus Charter 20 books, 4 *Bulletins* & 4 Translation books (£223, £265, £292)
Single copies £6
Cover Art Kirill Voronkov **Website** Ohmind.me

Supported using public funding by
ARTS COUNCIL ENGLAND

Poetry Book Society | Churchill House | 12 Mosley Street |
Newcastle upon Tyne | NE1 1DE | 0191 230 8100 | pbs@inpressbooks.co.uk
WWW.POETRYBOOKS.CO.UK

LETTER FROM THE PBS

It is lovely that Ilya Kaminsky, who read at the Newcastle Poetry Festival last year, is our Summer Choice with *Deaf Republic*, and we're delighted that Deryn Rees-Jones and Seán Hewitt, who will be taking part in this year's festival have also been included in the selections. The Summer *Bulletin* will just be landing as the festival and our Northern Poetry Symposium take place, so we hope to meet or have met some of you there!

A reminder that we have PBS Guest Selector Andrew McMillan standing in for Vidyan Ravinthiran in this *Bulletin* edition, and congratulations to Vidyan for his Recommendation selection. The poets in this *Bulletin* all write from completely different perspectives with a huge range of experience. We really hope you enjoy the features and are inspired to use your 25% membership discount to purchase their books.

We always love to hear our members' views on the latest selections and have launched a virtual poetry book club so you can discuss your favourites on social media using the hashtag #pbsonlinebookclub on Twitter @PoetryBookSoc. We also have a new bookclub discount rate, so if you'd like to start your own local poetry book club using the PBS Selections then do get in touch and we'll be happy to share the details with other members in your area. You can also check out our Vlogger in Residence Jen Campbell's latest video reviews on our website.

Please look out for the review of *This Tilting Earth* by Jane Lovell, winner of the PBS & Mslexia Women's Pamphlet Competition. We are delighted to be running the PBS & Mslexia Women's Poetry and Pamphlet competitions again, launching in June 2019, so if you are a female poet, we look forward to receiving your submissions. Keep a look out on our website for more details soon.

SOPHIE O'NEILL
PBS and Inpress Director

ILYA KAMINSKY

Ilya Kaminsky was born in the former Soviet Union and is now an American citizen. He is the author of *Dancing in Odessa* (Arc), and coeditor of *The Ecco Anthology of International Poetry*. He was a 2014 Finalist for the Neustadt International Prize for Literature. His other honours include a Guggenheim Fellowship, a Lannan Literary Fellowship, and a Whiting Award. His work has been translated into more than twenty languages.

DEAF REPUBLIC

FABER | £10.99 | PBS PRICE   £8.25

Ilya Kaminsky's second collection opens with a poem that may well be familiar even to those who don't know his work; 'We lived Happily during the War' went viral on the internet for its indictment of passivity in the face of conflict:

And when they bombed other people's houses, we protested
but not enough, we opposed them but not

enough…

What follows this brilliant opener is a cast list for the narrative drama we are about to bear witness to. The townspeople of Vasenka, and the military brutality which is about to be unleashed on them. Through short lyric snapshots of domestic love and sensuality, and harrowing narrative poems of violence and suppression, we are given an arresting and very moving collection.

Interspersed through the poems are images which give us the sign-language for certain words, such as "town" or "match"; giving the readers another language with which to interpret what is happening. The poems implicate us as readers in our positions as bystanders to the violence which we witness throughout the collection and what emerges as we read on is the collective resistance of silence; brutality in the poems is often connected to noise, the "police whistle" being one example, and the collection asks and re-asks how silence fits in to an act of collective resistance against an oppressive force.

Every so often, when we think we might be in the comforts of history, a long way away from where we are sat now, reading the book, an image like a woman being torn "from her bed like a door off a bus" reminds us that this is very much the present day.

In a note at the end of the collection the poet reminds us that "silence is the invention of the hearing"; so too freedom is most often defined by those who would seek to restrict it.

ANDREW McMILLAN

ILYA KAMINSKY

I did not have hearing aids until I was sixteen. As a deaf child, I experienced my country as a nation without sound. Only images. So how did a deaf child experience the USSR falling apart? I heard with my eyes.

Walking through this city, a deaf boy watched the people; their ears were open all the time, they had no lids. I was interested in what sounds might be like. The whooshing. The hissing. The whistle. The sound of keys turning in the lock, or water moving through the pipes two floors above us.

But what if the whole country was deaf like me? So that whenever a policeman's commands were uttered, no one could hear? These questions seem very relevant in America today. When Trump gives his State of the Union address, which is full of lies, wouldn't it be apt if his words landed on the deaf ears of a whole nation?

So my book *Deaf Republic* opens when the soldiers shoot and kill a deaf boy. The gunshot becomes the last thing the citizens hear – all go deaf as a protest, and their protest is coordinated by sign language. Although it is a story about a crisis – for me it is really a book of love lyrics. At the center of this country is a married couple, a child is born. And when the soldiers open fire at the women in the street, one of them says:

> I sit down to write and tell you what I know:
> a child learns the world by putting it in her mouth,
> a girl becomes a woman and a woman, earth.
> Body, they blame you for all things and they
> seek in the body what doesn't live in the body.

ILYA RECOMMENDS

I am mostly re-reading. Lyric poets I go back to a lot are Dickinson, Mandelstam, Celan and Vallejo. I love these poets because they reinvented the language, the syntax, in a way that showed me their love/hate relationship with it. I love how Mandelstam isn't always grammatically correct in Russian (of course he simply sees new grammar), how Dickinson wants to grasp from one line to another, skipping the politesse, using dashes as stairs to jump between floors, or how Celan combines words because German vocabulary didn't make the right ones for the grasp of human despair. I love, too, the three dots in the middle of lines in Vallejo, who knew that language wasn't enough – this is probably the case, at one moment in her or his life, with any lyric poet.

WE LIVED HAPPILY DURING THE WAR

And when they bombed other people's houses, we

protested
but not enough, we opposed them but not

enough. I was
in my bed, around my bed America

was falling: invisible house by invisible house by invisible house—

I took a chair outside and watched the sun.

In the sixth month
of a disastrous reign in the house of money

in the street of money in the city of money in the country of money,
our great country of money, we (forgive us)

lived happily during the war.

DEAFNESS, AN INSURGENCY, BEGINS

Our country woke up next morning and refused to hear soldiers.
    In the name of Petya, we refuse.
    At six a.m., when soldiers compliment girls in the alleyway, the girls slide by, pointing to their ears. At eight, the bakery door is shut in soldier Ivanoff's face, though he's their best customer. At ten, Momma Galya chalks NO ONE HEARS YOU on the gates of the soldiers' barracks.
    By eleven a.m., arrests begin.
    Our hearing doesn't weaken, but something silent in us strengthens.
    After curfew, families of the arrested hang homemade puppets out of their windows. The streets empty but for the squeaks of strings and the *tap tap*, against the buildings, of wooden fists and feet.

    In the ears of the town, snow falls.

Town

Image: Joshua Virasami

JAY BERNARD

Jay Bernard is the author of the pamphlets *Your Sign is Cuckoo, Girl* (Tall Lighthouse, 2008), *English Breakfast* (Math Paper Press, 2013) and *The Red and Yellow Nothing* (Ink Sweat & Tears Press, 2016), which was shortlisted for the Ted Hughes Award 2017. A film programmer at BFI Flare and an archivist at Statewatch, they also participated in The Complete Works II project in 2014, in which they were mentored by Kei Miller. Jay was a Foyle Young Poet of the Year in 2005 and a winner of SLAMbassadors UK spoken word championship. Their poems have been collected in *Voice Recognition: 21 Poets for the 21st Century* (Bloodaxe, 2009), *The Salt Book of Younger Poets* (Salt, 2011), *Ten: The New Wave* (Bloodaxe, 2014) and *Out of Bounds: British Black & Asian Poets* (Bloodaxe, 2014).

RECOMMENDATION

SURGE

CHATTO & WINDUS | £10.00 | PBS PRICE £7.50

Jay Bernard writes in their introductory preface (printed, right) to *Surge*, "Looking at the New Cross Fire made me stop thinking anything about myself, my body, or my heritage is in any way contradictory, and re-enforced the necessity of exploring black British history from a complex queer position." By focusing on a pivotal, but under-remembered, moment in history – the 1981 New Cross Fire that resulted in the deaths of fourteen young black Londoners – Bernard's book unlocks the complexities of subjectivity and memory for a modern-day readership. Informed by research during a residency at the George Padmore Institute in Finsbury Park, Bernard engages with both the gaps that inevitably emerge from an archive but also, crucially, they account for the enforced silences of marginalised histories. *Surge* redraws personal temporalities into a remarkably vivid portrait of race relations, of a history of violence and neglect, through multiple and often spectral voices. The complex subjectivity alluded to in Bernard's preface inhabits the book as an aesthetic deterritorialising of identity, making categories and poetic forms fluxive and responsive to the interstices in both individual voice and collective knowledge.

> don't you love that there is nothing
> remarkable here, nothing that would
> startle a state, but that it has been kept
> anyway, noted, dated, numbered, placed
> in acid-free Japanese boxes and lovingly
> (as is tradition) laid without a casket.

The book's opening poem, 'Arrival', is reminiscent of the poet and theorist Edouard Glissant's departure scene of a darkened sea-crossing from his nomadic work *The Poetics of Relation*, but here Bernard is standing on the opposite bank, a kind of home:

> remember we were brought here from the clear waters of our dreams
> that we might be named, numbered and forgotten.

Bernard pushes lyricism, its solipsism, to make an account for the self as inhabiting myriad voices through monologue, prose forms, disassembling the embeddedness of the "I" to point, brilliantly, towards our own collective accountability to remember.

SANDEEP PARMAR

I SELECTOR'S COMMENT

JAY BERNARD

On 2 March 1981, thousands of black people and their allies gathered at Fordham Park in Lewisham. It came to be known as the Black People's Day of Action and was the largest political gathering of black people in British history at the time. Organised by underacknowledged British activists such as John La Rose, Darcus Howe, Sybil Phoenix, Alex Pascall and many others, the intended route went from Lewisham to Hyde Park. It was raining. No demonstration had crossed a bridge in London for centuries. As the demonstration approached Blackfriars, the police tried to push the crowds back. People ran. This flowed into Fleet Street, once home of the media, where journalists leaned out of the windows and spat and jeered at the march. After a belated response to the deaths of the thirteen young people (addressed to the activists, not the families), a police initiative began in retaliation to the Black People's Day of Action, and ostensibly to curb crime in South London. The hated SUS laws gave licence to SWAMP 81, an operation in which close to a thousand black and ethnic minority people were stopped and searched in South London in five days. The name of the operation was seen as an insensitive reference to Thatcher's 1978 speech in which she said, "People are really rather afraid, that this country might be rather swamped by people with a different culture... people are going to react and be rather hostile to those coming in." During the tense time of SWAMP 81, the attempted arrest of a man who had been stabbed prompted the Brixton uprising in April 1981, also known as the Brixton riots. Since the blame for this lay firmly at the door of the police, an investigation was commissioned producing the Scarman Report, 'The Brixton Disorders 10–12 April 1981'; it found the police guilty of causing the riots due to its refusal to listen to the community it was supposed to serve. This triggered a new xi era in race relations in the UK, in conjunction with the ongoing activism and resistance of the black, Asian and ethnic minority organising groups. My residency began just after the Brexit vote. As I read through the interviews, looked at the photos, listened to the audio, watched the footage, it struck me that the events of the present were eerily similar to the events up to and after the New Cross Fire. Then in June 2017, Grenfell happened. Institutional indifference to working class lives had left nearly eighty people dead. The Windrush scandal was reminiscent of right-wing calls for black repatriation. The archive became, for me, a mirror of the present, a much-needed instruction manual to navigate what felt like the repetition of history. The most chilling aspect of this was the lack of closure, the lack of responsibility and the lack of accountability at the centre of both the New Cross Fire and Grenfell. And the more I read and discussed, the more vexed the relationship between public narration and private truths appeared. I realised I was one of many who had visited the archives and come to a similar conclusion about the tragic and ill-concluded nature of the case. Many questions emerged not only about memory and history, but about my place in Britain as a queer black person. This opened out into a final sense of coherence: I am from here, I am specific to this place, I am haunted by this history but I also haunt it back.

They call this a city, I call it dark between two bodies.

Image: Lily Jones

PEM-PEOPLE

We have come to light a candle for you
Naomi, at the pop-up shop in Peckham.

We lay out red and green cloth, fairy lights,
bring a steaming pot of beans to share.

A woman stands in the centre.
Your death, she says, proves

that there is no difference between the one
you love and the one who kills you.

A man in a grey suit speaks from his seat,
saying he knew you. He is angry, talking of how you

loved tennis, the Williams sisters
with their braids and their power, white-skirted

black thunder life-giving on the green.
He says you were as fierce as that.

Do we clap? Okay, we do. Then he asks for one
minute's silence above the evening traffic,

dancehall, the people in the room above us,
and it is silent here – the minute comes and

passes and still it is silent. I take a yellow
Post-it note and try to write something true

but really I am hungry and tired, really
I have nothing, really I want to eat the bean stew alone

and watch Venus throw her serve across YouTube
until it takes me somewhere I did not intend.

Image: Georgia Roach

ZOË BRIGLEY

Zoë Brigley grew up in Caerphilly in the Rhymney Valley of Wales, and is now an Assistant Professor at the Ohio State University in the US. She won an Eric Gregory Award in 2003 and received a Welsh Academy bursary in 2005. Her first book of poems, *The Secret* (Bloodaxe Books, 2007), was a Poetry Book Society Recommendation, and was longlisted for the Dylan Thomas Prize in 2008. Her second collection, *Conquest* (Bloodaxe Books, 2012), was also a Poetry Book Society Recommendation. A book of her non-fiction essays, *Notes from a Swing State*, is due from Parthian Books in 2019. She also researches violence against women, and is co-editor of a volume of scholarly essays, *Feminism, Literature, and Rape Narratives* (Routledge, 2010).

RECOMMENDATION

HAND & SKULL

BLOODAXE | £9.95 | PBS PRICE £7.47

ZOË BRIGLEY

HAND & SKULL

Among the epistolary voices of tragic literary heroines, *Hand & Skull* intersperses photographic works by the modernist photographer, Arthur Stieglitz, his wife the artist Georgia O'Keeffe, and gothic drawings by Victoria Brookland. These visuals, of O'Keeffe's hands with a horse's skull, and the darkly suggestive sublimations of desire and resistance in Brookland's work, punctuate the book's own lyric re-imaginings of the victims of male violence. For example, we find an Oulipian unfolding of the final section of Kate Chopin's turn-of-the-century novel, *The Awakening*, in 'Letter from Edna Pontellier'. The poem marvellously recasts the protagonist's unconscious drives:

> Don't mind what I'm saying: I am
> just thinking aloud under a white shawl.

The line break will certainly reverberate with anyone who knows the novel and its crisis, but those unfamiliar with Chopin (or indeed O'Keeffe and others) will sense the rising tension in each of Brigley's wronged women. In 'Letter from Georgia O'Keeffe' Brigley inhabits the tensions of their uneven partnership.

> He opened the lens – and I did as I was told –
> sat long and bare for the stretch of a four-minute
> exposure. A stormy night on Lake George – and later
> he wrote – *All is right between us for you gave me*
> *your virginity. You offered the very center.* And he hung
> me in pieces on his gallery wall. He is – I suspect
> – always photographing himself...

O'Keeffe and Stieglitz's marriage is put under the lens in several of these poems, transmuting the intimacies of their infamously mellifluous correspondence through the visual framing of O'Keeffe in her husband's photographs. Elsewhere, the photographic horse's skull wears the flesh of the personal, an upbringing in South Wales and the pagan horse-head-donning tradition of Mari Lwyd. Teenage suicide from economic privation infuse old rituals with their attendant and necessary senses of both loss and hope. What is clear and indeed most memorable about Brigley's dramatic monologues or epistolary poems, her weaving of narratives of violence, rape, even childbirth, is that the framing of the self undoes its own edges. In fact, it must continue to do so, in order to survive.

ZOË BRIGLEY

Hand & Skull mingles my own experiences of violence with tellings from real and imagined women. Mythical figures like Leda and Syrinx speak alongside letters from Tess of the D'Urbervilles, and Edna Pontellier (the self-destructive heroine of Kate Chopin's *The Awakening*). There are echoes of testimonies from real cases of violence against women, and this means including the voices of all kinds of women – not just white, straight, cisgender women. There are conversations with creators like Alun Lewis, Marina Tsvetaeva, and Georgia O'Keeffe.

The collection cover features O'Keeffe's painting, *Cow Skull with Calico Roses*, and there are images inside by my long-time collaborator Victoria Brookland, as well as Alfred Stieglitz's photograph of O'Keeffe's hands with a horse skull. O'Keeffe features throughout the collection, as do skulls: from O'Keeffe's paintings; from my childhood near farming country; skulls from Welsh myth and folk tradition; and the skull as a metaphor for an overwhelming and bleak sublime.

The hands of the title might be healing or harmful, but they represent the pull of the outside world. One epigraph quotes Edith Wharton's *The Age of Innocence*: "You knew, you understood; you felt the world tugging with all its golden hands." For better or worse, the world beckons, offering not only pain, but delight and joy. As Ann Cahill reminds us, the influence of violence inflicted on a person is "broad but not infinite."

Hands have the capacity to hurt, but they can also be the hands of a lover, of a friend, a child reaching out. Later poems in the collection try to capture – in an honest way – the strange and moving experience of childbearing, admitting how precarious the process can be. Despite how it begins, the whole collection is journeying towards joy.

ZOË RECOMMENDS

Ruth Awad, *Set to Music a Wildfire* (Southern Indiana Review Press, 2017); Robin Coste Lewis, *Voyage of the Sable Venus* (Knopf, 2015); Carrie Etter, *The Weather in Normal* (Seren, 2018); Kathy Fagan, *Sycamore* (Milkweed, 2017); Vievee Francis, *Forest Primeval* (Northwestern Uni Press, 2015); Bhanu Kapil, *Ban en Banlieue* (Nightboat, 2015); Joanna Klink, *Raptus* (Penguin, 2010); Amy King, *I Want to Make You Safe* (Litmus, 2011); Khaty Xiong, *Poor Anima* (Apogee, 2015); Maggie Smith, *The Well Speaks of its Own Poison* (Tupelo).

now you are walking out into the light

Image: *Vésuviennes*, Victoria Brookland

LETTER FROM TESS DURBEYFIELD

I am always brave
on long walks home: the wet lane: tender steps over
waters which break the gully banks, and cross
the path in shiny, grey fingers: ribbons
lacing. I walk, even when
stretches of land open like an empty
stomach. The chestnut trees were lopped one
by one to stumps: first platforms for children to raise
fists and clamour, later nothing but a dull spot
amongst the sharper green. I pass, and
by the knobbly hesitation of my limbs, by my straight,
pretty body, and the bright swing
of my hair, I know myself exactly. I feel myself
blank and longing under my schoolgirl coat.
No one could know how I hate it. In my pocket,
chestnuts the colour of hide, the shade
of a thoroughbred, though marred
by a spot of white that might
be an eye or navel. I don't know
it now, but I am about
to bend. The snap of a branch, or bone
under a human hand.

DERYN REES-JONES

Deryn Rees-Jones works as a poet, editor and critic. She won an Eric Gregory award in 1993 and *The Memory Tray* (Seren, 1995) was shortlisted for the Forward Prize for Best First Collection. Her other works are *Signs Round a Dead Body* (Seren, 1998), *Quiver* (Seren, 2004), and a ground-breaking critical study of twentieth-century women's poetry, *Consorting with Angels* (Bloodaxe, 2005), published alongside *Modern Women Poets* (Bloodaxe, 2005). She is Professor of Poetry at Liverpool University, and editor of the poetry series for Pavilion Press at Liverpool University Press.

ERATO

SEREN | £9.99 | PBS PRICE £7.50

Erato

Deryn Rees-Jones

"...an elegy-haunted celebration of the rich interchangeability of concepts and images..." - *Carol Rumens*, The Guardian

Much is often made (quite rightly) of the exciting and energetic new voices which emerge into poetry each year. But what of the voices who have been working at deepening, strengthening and expanding their art over many years? Deryn Rees-Jones' new collection is at once a firm continuation of her singular poetic project and a lightning strike which takes both her work and us as readers into utterly unfamiliar territory.

I'm reminded of what Ian Duhig said of Rees-Jones' *Burying The Wren* (Seren, 2012), that it was a collection which marked "an important development in her work"; the same could be said of this collection and yet development seems too mild a word. Rather a departure, a rupture, a new beginning.

This is a formally varied collection; long prose explorations side by side with Haiku-like glimpses. In the first of the prose pieces, indeed the book's opener, 'Mon Amour', Rees-Jones writes: "Yet all landscapes I held within me seemed to be receding". That seems key to unlocking this work, something long held within, finally let go of, and something new emerging in its place. That opening poem ends with a paradox, that dual-sense of both an ending and a new beginning is what makes this collection so exciting and moving.

Something I knew was only beginning.
Something, I knew, was at an end

There are poems here of nature, of birds, of the body; poems which are tender to the wider world, not just to the physical self. There are poems which are small and intimate and, in 'Walk' in particular, poems which speak to the world and its geo-political state. This is a book which is always looking towards something new, the old ways, the old forms, the contended lyric, is not enough anymore (or so this book seems to suggest) and so there is a reaching out, of the line, of the image, in order to try and grasp something which might be just beyond reach, but which the poems will keep trying to move towards.

I wanted to be light, light as air.

ANDREW McMILLAN

DERYN REES-JONES

At the beginning of Book Seven of the *Aeneid*, Virgil evokes the muse of love and lyric poetry, Erato, as he begins to write about war and the rebuilding of a nation. Many scholars have commented on the strangeness of such an invocation. But it is a strangeness I rely on here in an attempt to ask searching questions – and perhaps unanswerable ones – of myself and of poetry, as I explore the relationship between personal grief and global events, and love's work in rebuilding a relationship between self and world.

Burying the Wren (2012), my last book, took as an epigraph lines from Roethke's 'In a Dark Time'. That was a book about the transformations of motherhood, as well as a book that began to touch on the experience of losing a husband and bringing up two young children in the shadows of that loss. *Erato* takes up those threads, in a silent return to Roethke's poem, when he asks "Which I is I?" So poems and ideas are repeated and returned to in various forms – prose poems, more directly autobiographical documents of experiences in my life, and the rawness of autobiography transformed in the music of lyric.

I think of *Erato* as an optimistic book, one that believes in beauty and in poetry, but one which is also unafraid of challenging those categories to accommodate the ugly and the violent feelings. And even as the book plays with ideas of error and slippage, the inevitable errata of memory, its misinformation and reinscriptions, it also tries to find a way to accommodate the spaces in between the known and the unknown. *Erato* is a book full of fires and flames. It is a book of passions, and one which ultimately believes, as Virginia Woolf writes in her book about the coming into being of a woman poet, *Orlando*, that poetry is "a voice answering a voice".

DERYN RECOMMENDS

Bhanu Kapil, *Schizophrene* (Nightboat, 2011) and *Ban et Banlieu* (Nightboat, 2015); *The Collected Stories of Lydia Davis* (Penguin, 2014); Seamus Heaney, *Field Work* (Faber, 1979); Elizabeth Bishop, *Poems, Prose and Letters* (Library of America, 2008); Thomas Traherne, via the poetryfoundation.org website; Forrest Gander, *Be With* (New Directions, 2018); Virgil, *The Aeneid*, trans. Robert Fagles (Penguin, 2010).

We were all error,

slippage. You were a song and its singing...

ERRATUM

Peter, 3.5

We had driven to the woods. Only a walker, occasional, nosed the world's corners. You pulled me down: mud, leaf-mulch, moving shade and shadow.

Let me start again. You took my hand and we agreed. We'd walked the long way to the burning copse. I saw myself being set alight, my face blackened to a shroud of bees. Look up, I said, the sky splintering through evergreens. You were bending me slowly, then, across a fallen tree trunk. We were all error,

slippage. You were a song and its singing. We were a burning corpse. Or was it the light, those soft explosions, blowing us open a note in the breeze. Do you recall? Your coat was a bear-skin on the young wet grass. I thought of Blodeuwedd and her face of flowers. I remembered silence that was never a silence; the woods inching into being around us, the green powder of algae from treebark, staining my cheeks, my lips, my hands, my knees.

VIDYAN RAVINTHIRAN

Vidyan Ravinthiran's first collection *Grun-tu-molani* (Bloodaxe, 2014) was shortlisted for several prizes; poems from his second won a Northern Writers' Award. His critical study *Elizabeth Bishop's Prosaic* (Bucknell, 2015) won both the University English Prize and the Warren-Brooks Award for Outstanding Literary Criticism. He is also a winner of Poetry's Editors' Prize for Reviewing and has worked with the Prince's Trust, the British Council and New Writing North. Vidyan comes from a family of Sri Lankan Tamils and his heritage informs his verse, criticism and also the fiction he has begun to write.

THE MILLION-PETALLED FLOWER OF BEING HERE

BLOODAXE | £9.95 | PBS PRICE £7.47

In the ninety-eight sonnets which make up this second collection we are given a truth so directly that we curse ourselves for not having thought of it previously: that the sonnet may well be the ideal form for capturing the contemporary moment. Here the traditional rubs up against the hyper-contemporary, in brilliant phrases like:

> My hangover is like a smashed windscreen

Or in 'Aubade':

> The sound of the curtains yanked apart
> is the morning clearing its throat

Through these beautiful poems of love and the domestic, we encounter the wider world; its racism, its parents, its day-to-day minutiae of living. Within the frame (should that be cage?) of the sonnet, a constant tension is created between a yearning across distance, between the precarity of the modern-day rental-market, fleeting encounters with strangers, and the solidity which the form offers up.

There are no cheap gimmicks here, no easy wins, just well-worked and heartfelt poems, which become erotic and sensual through their focused gaze on a life and another person; the voltas within the sonnets often bring in other scenes, other moments to the poems, showing us how memory and thought are often collages of different ideas.

There is violence lurking here too, a history which keeps threatening to break out from the tight lines and, alongside love, we are asked to consider the value of art, and of politics as well; the ultimate effect and feeling is one of radical sincerity as we move through the collection.

Larkin, who gives this collection its title, was a poet who was never afraid to reach towards "Poetry", towards the transcendent truth of the perfectly-selected image. He does not go un-critiqued within this collection, but this is a collection with that same sincere belief in the power of language to capture a feeling precisely.

ANDREW McMILLAN

VIDYAN RAVINTHIRAN

I always thought I'd become a weirder, more experimental poet as I went on. But that didn't happen, and sometimes you've got to write what comes to you, and through you, rather than persist with the original plan. I began writing sonnets to my wife, privately – they genuinely were for her ears only. It was a time in my life when I didn't feel confident of being listened to, I didn't know if my voice would carry outside our home. Gradually I realised some of these poems (not all of them) might interest others too. My title is from Philip Larkin, who uses the pronoun "we" unanxiously, feeling he can speak, if not universally, then at least on behalf of a community. Which is harder to assume these days. But what I've tried is to enlarge that pronoun beyond the situation of two people in love, so that readers of whatever background (this is a book concerned with race, gender and class) might feel included.

I decided to organise the book with two sonnets to a page, so poems themselves could enter into communication. I did worry about writing to a woman who remains silent: a Muse-figure and not a person. Men have been doing this for centuries. But if anyone wants Jenny Holden's thoughts, they can read her award-winning fiction or talk to her, and be enlivened and transformed, as I have been. (Well, okay, not to the same extent: hands off my wife!) On the back of the book you'll find her depiction, and transformation, of a detail from the woodcut on the cover: a picture of the two of us. So at least a sliver of her creativity emerges here. And there's one poem, about miscarriage, in which I had to include something beautiful, and supportive, and brave, which she said to me: "This is happening to you too."

VIDYAN RECOMMENDS

Dom Moraes was an Indian who moved to England and wrote brilliant formal verse. At his best there's a feeling of interlocking finality, of purely crystallised insight: "Quietly I move inside / the ferned cave of the word". E. Pauline Johnson, or *Tekahionwake*, was a 19th century Canadian poet whose father was Mohawk. Here's an extract from 'Shadow River: Muskoka':

> The little fern-leaf, bending
> Upon the brink, its green reflection greets,
> And kisses soft the shadow that it meets
> With touch so fine,
> The border line
> The keenest vision can't define;
> So perfect is the blending.

The flower of tomorrow is yet to open

TODAY

I was reading my book by the window
waiting for you when I noticed one flower
of those you'd artfully splayed had snapped.
Like a limp wrist the orange gerbera hung, and over
my knuckle it vented a beige gunge. As I snipped
the stem for a smaller vase, the glow
of the radiant petals was too much. Time lapped
me round, the day went unseized.
For this was no opportunity I could have missed;
only the lonely moment which blazed
in my hand, unplucked. Like many,
I had forgotten that time isn't money
and I don't need always to be on the move
within the world you've shown me how to love.

Image: Nancy Nichols

LAYLI LONG SOLDIER

Layli Long Soldier earned a BFA from the Institute of American Indian Arts and an MFA with honours from Bard College. She is the author of the chapbook *Chromosomory* and the collection *Whereas*. She has been a contributing editor to *Drunken Boat* and poetry editor at Kore Press. In 2012, her participatory installation, *Whereas We Respond*, was featured on the Pine Ridge Reservation. In 2015, Long Soldier was awarded a National Artist Fellowship from the Native Arts and Cultures Foundation and a Lannan Literary Fellowship for Poetry. She was awarded a Whiting Writer's Award in 2016. Long Soldier is a citizen of the Oglala Lakota Nation and lives in Santa Fe, New Mexico.

SPECIAL COMMENDATION

WHEREAS

PICADOR | £10.99 | PBS PRICE £8.25

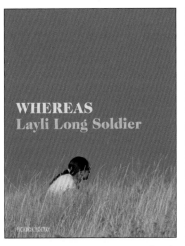

In the opening poem of *Whereas* is a square made up of variants of the phrase: "This is how you see me the space in which to place me". Each important variation brings the reader into an implicit subject position – placing, in space, the you and the me within the intimacies of language and relation. For Long Soldier, this question of how we see and place ourselves through language is inherently rooted in the United States' history of genocide against Native Americans, but also elsewhere in the continuous questioning of selfhood through a dissembling of the "I". Long Soldier writes that she is a citizen of both the US and of the Oglala Lakota Nation: "and in this dual citizenship, I must work, I must eat, I must art, I must mother, I must friend, I must listen, I must observe, constantly, I must live."

Long Soldier's poetics, her expansion of lyricism, her use of documentary methods, her engagement with pre-existing texts show an extraordinary emotional and intellectual depth that is, frankly, uncommon and much needed. *Whereas* is already a lauded and admired book in America, where the political questions about ethno-nationalist capitalism Long Soldier raises are fast becoming more febrile than ever. The most remarkable poems in her book are '38', a narrative that questions syntactically and formally its own limits, and the long eponymous sequence which finishes the book. '38' presupposes the trickery of language, particularly that of treaties used to drive Native Americans off their ancestral lands by the European settlers. 'Whereas' takes similar steps, and is a thrilling indictment of a symbolic Congressional apology to Native Americans in 2009. Long Soldier's sequence drills down into the gaps within official language, and each poem, or 'Whereas Statement', is wrought utterly through the self's relationship to language and its accountability.

> If I'm transformed by language, I am often
> crouched in footnote or blazing in title.
> Where in the body do I begin;

In our current historical moment, in which language is devalued and denatured particularly by violence, otherness and hate, Long Soldier's ethical rejoinder and her recontextualising of responsibility is absolutely crucial to us all.

SANDEEP PARMAR

SELECTOR'S COMMENT

WHEREAS

WHEREAS the word *whereas* means it being the case that, or considering that, or while on the contrary; is a qualifying or introductory statement, a conjunction, a connector. Whereas sets the table. The cloth. The saltshakers and plates. Whereas calls me to the table. Whereas precedes and invites. I have come now. I'm seated across from a Whereas smile. Under pressure of formalities, I fidget I shake my legs. I'm not one for these smiles, Whereas I have spent my life in unholding. *What do you mean by unholding?* Whereas asks and since Whereas rarely asks, I am moved to respond, Whereas, I have learned to exist and exist without your formality, saltshakers, plates, cloth. Without the slightest conjunctions to connect me. Without an exchange of questions, without the courtesy of answers. It is mine, this unholding, so that with or without the setup, I can see the dish being served. Whereas let us bow our heads in prayer now, just enough to eat;

LIEKE MARSMAN

Lieke Marsman is the author of two full-length collections of poetry, *Watik mijzelf graag voorhoud, Things I Tell Myself*, and *De eerste letter, The First Letter*, for which she has received several awards, including the C. Buddingh' Award and the Van der Hoogt Prize. Her first novel, *Het tegenovergestelde van een mens, The Opposite of a Person*, which incorporates poetry and non-fiction to address questions of climate change and loneliness, was published in 2017 by Atlas Contact.

Sophie Collins grew up in Bergen, North Holland, and now lives in Edinburgh. *small white monkeys*, a text on self-expression, self-help and shame, was published by Book Works in 2017 as part of a commissioned residency at Glasgow Women's Library. Her first collection of poems *Who Is Mary Sue?* was published by Faber and was the PBS Spring 2018 Choice.

THE FOLLOWING SCAN WILL LAST FIVE MINUTES
LIEKE MARSMAN, TRANSLATED BY SOPHIE COLLINS
PAVILION | £9.99 | PBS PRICE £7.50

The Following Scan Will Last Five Minutes

LIEKE MARSMAN

TRANSLATED BY SOPHIE COLLINS

There is poetry and there are its various subjects, including itself. Some things, one might argue, lie beyond the scope of poetry, being too direct, too immediate, not yet absorbed into the matrix of language, too much a cry or a report, not the thing itself because the thing is too big, too present. Cancer, they might argue, is one of those. In 1984 Peter Reading published his book *C*, a hundred poems in a hundred words each charting a hundred days, ranging from prose to virtuosic classical metres. It is a bruising yet beautiful work.

The Dutch poet Lieke Marsman's poems in *The Following Scan Will Last Five Minutes*, including a central section of prose in the form of a response to Audre Lorde's *The Cancer Journals*, begin and end in verse but are then followed by a series of letters from her translator, Sophie Collins. The book is very much in dialogue with Lorde, with Collins, with Marsman herself all in a political context – a capsule of interconnections. The poems speak plainly and think plainly and that is their power as translated by Collins, but their effect is to offer a multi-dimensional set of reports, contemplations and intense but underplayed tensions. It isn't a normal book of poetry, but it is certainly poetry and despite its plainness and nakedness there is little like it.

The other book that particularly tempted me was Pere Gimferrer's *The Catalan Poems*, translated by Adrian Nathan West. *The Catalan Poems* is as different as it's possible to be. Marsman begins and ends with the situation that is its cause and focus, Gimferrer with Apollinaire, Juan Gris and Hölderlin. His epigraph to his first poem quotes Wallace Stevens: "Poetry is the subject of the poem". The poems themselves are the argument for this. They are referential, full of sharp imagery, always aware of their position as objects. Poetry, he says is:

> a system of rotating
> mirrors, gliding harmoniously,
> displacing light and shadow in the mutable room: why
> the frosted glass? ...

With Gimferrer we are in the mutable room: with Marsman in the cancer ward.

GEORGE SZIRTES

SELECTOR'S COMMENT

THE FOLLOWING SCAN WILL LAST LESS THAN A MINUTE

afternoons are
Eurosport replays
of alpine skiing
sponsored by Jack Wolfskin and Milka
brands to whom I am grateful
for facilitating this daily moment of calm

evenings are the joy
I take in loving Simone as much as I do
especially in the face of this overwhelming exhaustion

cancer is so quotidian
you hear about it on Wednesday morning
die on a Tuesday afternoon
no strobe lights
no cloakroom check-in
the sun is shining
a completely ordinary insipid sun
above the A10
and the exit for Praxis

LIEKE MARSMAN

41

Image: Rory Lewis

SEÁN HEWITT

Seán Hewitt was born in 1990 and read English at the University of Cambridge, where he received his college's Emily Davies and Lilias Sophia Ashworth Hallett scholarships and twice received the Charity Reeves Prize in English. In 2014, he was awarded Arts Council England funding for a series of poems, and in 2015 was selected as one of the Poetry Trust's Aldeburgh Eight. He has read at Ilkley Literature Festival, Durham Book Festival and Aldeburgh Poetry Festival, and has taught creative writing at Liverpool John Moores University. He is a fiction reviewer for *The Irish Times* and a Leverhulme Research Fellow at Trinity College, Dublin. He won a Northern Writers' Award in 2016, and the Resurgence Prize in 2017.

LANTERN

OFFORD   ROAD   BOOKS | £6.00

It's rare to come across a debut this assured, especially one published by a relatively new press (Offord Road Books), but Seán Hewitt's debut *Lantern* is stunning. It opens with 'Leaf', a reflection on grief, which sets the tone for a collection that uses nature to deal with themes ranging from love and loss to faith and violence. These poems make you deeply aware of the fragile nature of our existence and how, despite ourselves, we are connected to the world around us and centred by it.

Lantern contains several longer poems and Hewitt displays real skill in sustaining the momentum required to keep the reader's attention, surprising you at each turn. In 'Dryad', the speaker recounts a sexual awakening that places him at the heart of a natural landscape:

> I came here with a man whose whole body
> was muscled, as though he too had been carved
> from a single trunk of wood.

In 'Kyrie', the speaker tries to find the source of "a moaning, // a pain riddling from the undergrowth, / a voice caught out after dark" and finds himself "at a place / so close to life, to its truth of violence". The title, 'Kyrie', turns the poem into a prayer, and religious imagery runs through several other poems too. In 'Petition', the act of faith and renewal is seen as a way "to reassemble my life around me […] to see myself shattered / and remade, if only to show myself / that this is possible".

Lantern is exquisite. It contains every human experience, placing it within the context of the natural landscape so that you can find your way even when life feels out of control and hard to understand. It makes you feel that despite living in a world full of fear and death and violence, there is always hope. It's a collection that you'll keep coming back to, whenever you need light in dark times.

> I turn home, and all across the floor
> the spiked white flowers
> light the way. The world is dark
> but the wood is full of stars.

A.B. JACKSON & DEGNA STONE

LEAF

for woods are forms of grief
grown from the earth. for they creak

with the weight of it.
for each tree is an altar to time.

for the oak, whose every knot
guards a hushed cymbal of water.

for how the silver water holds
the heavens in its eye.

for the axletree of heaven
and the sleeping coil of wind

and the moon keeping watch.
for how each leaf traps light as it falls.

for even in the nighttime of life
it is worth living, just hold it.

SEÁN HEWITT

Image: Andy Lo Pó

INUA ELLAMS

Born in Nigeria, Inua Ellams is a cross art form practitioner; a poet, playwright, performer, graphic artist, designer and founder of the Midnight Run – an international, arts-filled, night-time, playful, urban walking experience. He is a Complete Works poet alumnus and a designer at White Space Creative Agency. Across his work, identity, displacement and destiny are recurring themes in which he also tries to mix the old with the new: traditional African storytelling with contemporary poetry, and pencil with pixel. His poetry is published by Flipped Eye, Akashic, Nine Arches and several plays by Oberon.

THE HALF GOD OF RAINFALL

HARPER COLLINS | £10.00 | PBS PRICE £7.50 HB

INUA ELLAMS

The world Inua Ellams conjures in his verse-novel *The Half God of Rainfall* boldly experiments with classical and contemporary modes of poetry and storytelling. Part Homeric fantasy, part a Tarantino-esque blockbuster, the plot follows a precocious basketball player who we learn is:

"Half Grecian God. Half-child of Zeus. Half lord of river waters. He would grow to possess odd gifts."

Written in Europe's famous hexametrical *terza rima* – six feet and A-B-A B-C-B rhyme scheme, the book weaves a highly imagined narrative with a fine-tuned poetic register, typified in the opening stanza:

"The local boys had chosen grounds not too far from the river so a cooled breeze could blow them twisting in the heat."

Split into three Acts, again division presents itself as a clear agenda for Ellams, we are thrown between the dichotomy of perceived realities. The decadent steeps of the Greek Gods, where they connive and bicker among each other, to that of worldly humans where love, vulnerability, friendship and competition all conspire through basketball teams and their lionised players:

"Much like a match struck in full sunlight is how mortals look before the clout of Gods."

In all the high-camp delineation of Gods versus mortals versus superhuman power, Ellams' work has a larger and more complex preoccupation than that of simply refashioning famous plots. Power and patriarchy are his fundamental concerns. With this in mind *The Half God of Rainfall* comes as a timely reproach levelled against the way certain masculinities have impacted upon women within society. Having the text anchored in ancient Greek mythos while reimagining those characters in modern times leaves the reader seriously questioning current power structures, the barbarity of gender-based violence and what it means to survive such atrocities.

SELECTOR'S COMMENT

ANTHONY ANAXAGOROU

INUA ELLAMS

In 2011, when attending Roddy Lumsden's class at the Poetry School, I shared a poem called 'Of All the boys of Plateau Private School' in which I describe a schoolboy friend whose party trick was to spit saliva into the air as high as he could and then catch it in his mouth. I called him "The Half God of Rainfall". Roddy said he liked the image and in the weeks after, I began to interrogate it.

In basketball, which I play, terribly, great shooters are said to "make it rain" on the court and I imagined a great three point shooter, so good, he seemed supernatural. I wondered if indeed he could be, and the "half" in his title could suggest a cultural hybridity? Could he be part Nigerian and part... English? No. Part Greek. A Greek God. Perhaps Zeus could be his father? I began looking into Zeus as a father figure, into his relationship with his children and their mothers and discovered stories that hadn't been shared with me when I first encountered the Olympians as a child. The stories showed that, without a doubt, Zeus was a serial sex offender. As soon as I voiced that to myself, I felt something akin to blasphemy. Could I think that about such a looming figure? What would this mean for my Half God?

I was born into a Muslim and Christian household, into a multiplicity of faith and belief systems, so I had questioned religions for as long as I could remember but this felt like a personal betrayal. Whenever I had read the Quran or the Bible, there were historical and factual stakes raised in how I received the text, indeed my eternal soul was on the line. But I enjoyed the Greek Myths as fantastic stories. I allowed them into me as pure entertainment, without filters, where good was good and bad was bad, but realising this about Zeus meant something deceitful and disgusting nestled at its heart.

I dug into the Orisha deities of the Ifá faith of the Yoruba people of West Africa and discovered power-structural parallels between them and the Olympians. I saw how it affected and afflicted the goddesses and mortal women, and in that the kindling for the story was lit. *The Half God of Rainfall* is a new epic myth which begins on a tiny grassy basketball court in south west Nigeria and comes to the 2012 Olympics in London, via the furthest reaches of our solar system. It is about contemporary faith, power, revenge and female solidarity.

INUA RECOMMENDS

I'd like to recommend *Hoops* by Major Jackson, published in 2006. I read it three years later on Jacob Sam-La Rose's recommendation. I had never encountered basketball in verse and Major wrote with an art director's clarity and precision, music and love, such that I could smell the sweat off the asphalt, off the ballers, the beer on their breath as they insulted each other on inner city basketball courts. I come to it like a favourite film, re-living its twists and turns for pure pleasure.

SUMMER BOOK REVIEWS

An expansive range of poetry from assorted projects and commissions comes together under one roof, demonstrating the breadth of Armitage's interests and abilities. Here you will find meditations upon war and remembrance, studies of landscapes and countryside, responses to classical literature, sculpture, travel, history and more. *Sandettie Light Vessel Automatic* is both playful and thought-provoking, accessible and evocative. A wonderful volume for the Armitage enthusiast or those approaching his work for the first time.

FABER & FABER | £16.99 HB | PBS PRICE £12.75

The second collection by this Forward Prize winning poet examines the aftermath of grief with poignant exactitude. Ranging from Tankas to Ghazals, this is a protean collection, absorbing numerous forms and cultures: "I've begun to turn porous again". Gods big and small weave in and out of these lyrical invocations, from the Hindu Draupadi to mythic Odysseus. Although "mostly waiting for rain", Arshi leads us towards light and hope in poems that are both "arboreal and free".

PAVILION POETRY | £9.99 | PBS PRICE £7.50

PBS Vlogger-in-Residence Jen Campbell's debut poetry collection is suffused with the carnivalesque. Following in the footsteps of writers such as Angela Carter, *The Girl Aquarium* describes bodies in flux – metamorphosis, inversion and immersion, consuming and being consumed. Campbell also returns to her roots, inhabiting the voices of North-Eastern women, stirring the dialect into a heady mix of fairy-tale inheritances. You can watch Jen's video reviews of all the PBS selections on Youtube.

BLOODAXE | £9.95 | PBS PRICE £7.47

SKIN CAN HOLD: VAHNI CAPILDEO

Skin Can Hold presents the ever-erudite Vahni Capildeo at their signature best: "Customers (or indeed readers) may be deemed to require a cranial refitting". Surreal "playlets" on Muriel Spark sit alongside "Hamlet Oulipo", experimental "ablutions" and performances with stage directions. Capildeo revels in word–play and existential questioning, "the end of the poem happened before it began", with treatises on shame, gender, and erasure, combining insatiable curiosity and linguistic ingenuity.

CARCANET | £9.99 | PBS PRICE £7.50

WHEN I GROW UP I WANT TO BE A LIST OF FURTHER POSSIBILITIES: CHEN CHEN

A fierce debut collection by an exciting new Asian-American poet who unflinchingly explores the "immigrant queer" experience. Bursting with love and loss, the erotic and the politic, as the US poetry giant Jericho Brown claims, "Chen is a poet I will be reading for the rest of my life". Chen's quirky imagery celebrates the curious oddity of the everyday, "dreaming of one day being as fearless as a mango", and leaves us brimming with possibilites.

BLOODAXE | £9.95 | PBS PRICE £7.47

DOUBLE NEGATIVE: VONA GROARKE

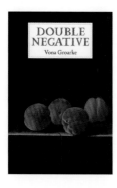

This seventh collection by the leading Irish poet Vona Groarke hinges upon the doubleness of daily life: "a day without a volta / is a day with nowhere to hide". Poems pivot from witty observations about doilies or Charlotte Brontë's underwear to images of aching loss: "my body, grief colander". Memory, the past and shifting certainties underpin these poems "against" darkness, each writing a way, through double negatives, to positivity.

THE GALLERY PRESS | £10.50 | PBS PRICE £7.88

SUMMER BOOK REVIEWS

THE UNKNOWN NERUDA: PABLO NERUDA
TRANSLATED BY ADAM FEINSTEIN

A diverse collection of Nobel Prize winner Pablo Neruda's work, discovered in Chile in 2014. Drawing inspiration from both the everyday and banal, Neruda's emotive language gilds each line. From sombre to joyous, this collection takes us on a journey through love, loss and life. 'When, Chile?', a four-page ode to his homeland, is a poignant highlight of the book.

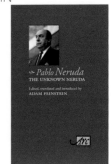

ARC | £10.99 | PBS PRICE £8.25

ROCK, PAPER, SCISSORS: RICHARD OSMOND

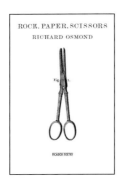

In a radical departure from the herbalism of his debut collection, Richard Osmond begins with the following statement: "On June 3rd 2017 I was out drinking with friends in the London Bridge / Borough Market area of London when a van was deliberately driven into pedestrians on London Bridge". Interweaving his eye witness experiences with fragments of the Quran and translations of Beowulf, this is a harrowing reflection on the complexities of terror, trauma and translation itself.

PICADOR | £10.99 | PBS PRICE £8.25

CRASH & BURN: MICHAEL O'NEILL

A fitting tribute to the distinguished poet, academic and recent PBS Special Commendation who sadly passed away earlier this year, *Crash & Burn* outlines the poet's own treatment for cancer with unflinching honesty. These hauntingly brave and beautiful poems remind us of the fragility of life: "the humdrum miracle of / being here still, writing another line". O'Neill's final posthumous collection, honours his lifelong dedication to poetry and lasting literary legacy.

ARC | £9.99 | PBS PRICE £7.50

WHIP-HOT & GRIPPY: HEATHER PHILLIPSON

This internationally renowned artist and poet presents an innovative collision of genres which raises playful and powerful questions about our world: "we're this close to checking out of planet earth". Part poem, part art installation, the final sequence connects words and images in a smartphone age where "context is nothing". Overcharged with imagery, this is a hyper-sensory experience, full of "melted cheese and destruction": an "extreme close-up / of the world oozing in at the edge".

BLOODAXE | £12.00 | PBS PRICE £9.00

THE INCENDIARY ART: PATRICIA SMITH

Patricia Smith's tour de force is dedicated to "every woman who began her morning with a son and ended the day without one." A chronicle of endemic violence against black communities in the US, Smith opens with the murder of the boy Emmett Till and storms through a century of murders to the modern age of Black Lives Matter. Every verse aches with mourning, every line powerfully composed. A haunting and necessary work.

BLOODAXE | £12.00 | PBS PRICE £9.00

THE LAUREATE'S CHOICE ANTHOLOGY

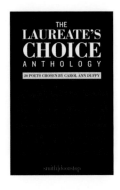

This is the definitive collection of twenty talented emerging poets, specially selected by the exiting UK Poet Laureate Carol Ann Duffy. Hera Lindsay Bird, Geraldine Clarkson, Keith Hutson and Greg Gilbert are among the poets featured in this eclectic and highly enjoyable selection. The anthology is further complemented by short essays from each of the poets explicating their work.

SMITH | DOORSTOP | £10.00 | PBS PRICE £7.50

BOOK REVIEWS

SUMMER PAMPHLETS

IN RETAIL: JEREMY DIXON

A familiar, cathartic reading experience for those who have worked in retail, many of the poems in this deeply funny collection began life jotted on the back of till-roll when Dixon worked for a chain of chemists. Treading the line between wry absurdism and abject despair, *In Retail* is like reading anthropological field-notes from what should be an alien world but is, unfortunately, our own.

ARACHNE   PRESS | £8.99 |

LOVE MAKES A MESS OF DYING: GREG GILBERT

This laureate-selected pamphlet covers the first year following Gilbert's cancer prognosis. As a singer and musician, Gilbert does not simply bring a lyrical quality to his poetry, but engages in various formal experiments – 'Blue-Draped Cube' treads the line between flash-fiction and prose-poem. This is an emotional journey about understanding not only the nature of death, but of coming to a deeper understanding of life and of love.

SMITH | DOORSTOP | £7.50 |

THIS TILTING EARTH: JANE LOVELL

Winner of this year's Mslexia and PBS Women's Pamphlet Competition, judged by Seren's Poetry Editor Amy Wack, *This Tilting Earth* presents a sequence of beautifully crafted poems about our out-of-kilter world. Lovell's poetry is poised between the elements, "I am curved air / or water over stone", and hinges upon natural "spill-points". The title poem considers tiny bones, tusks and vertebrae in a "song of lost species" which opens up the collection to wider ecological concerns about the future.

SEREN | £5.00 |

THE NEIGHBOURHOOD: HANNAH LOWE

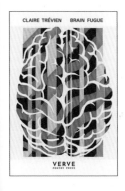

From gentrification to deportation, Lowe explores the changing face of neighbourhoods, urban spaces and community. Tales of recent refugee crises and red hot summers play out against the aptly named "multi-storey" and the increasingly casual horror of inner city life, "one boy shot dead another?" Laced with memories of family, fathers, childbirth and motherhood, Lowe maps the complex nexus of domestic and urban, circling around our own fragile yet familiar sense of home.

OUTSPOKEN   PRESS | £6.00 |

ELASTIC GLUE: KATHY PIMLOTT

Kathy Pimlott illustrates the way we as humans are affected by the places around us, expressing her views in an intense new light through a range of unique locations. From London to Sweden, Pimlott captures the pulse of place and the beating of the "city's glitzy heart". With a mix of strong emotions and vivid imagery, *Elastic Glue* is an incredible pamphlet which will enhance your perception of the world around you.

EMMA   PRESS | £6.50 |

BRAIN FUGUE: CLAIRE TRÉVIEN

The third in Verve Press' Experimental Pamphlet Series, *Brain Fugue* explores the brain in a variety of guises, as a city, a museum, as all and nothing. Trévien examines the mind at work, the cranial complexity of living between two languages and the duality of mental health: "My sadness is sick, my sickness is sad". This is an innovative and surreal sequence of poems which will certainly get you thinking...

VERVE   PRESS | £7.50 |

SUMMER LISTINGS
NEW BOOKS

AUTHOR	TITLE	PUBLISHER	RRP
Simon Armitage	Sandettie Light Vessel Automatic	Faber & Faber	£16.99
Mona Arshi	Dear Big Gods	Pavilion Poetry	£9.99
Zohar Atkins	Nineveh	Carcanet Press	£9.99
Janette Ayachi	Hand Over Mouth Music	Pavilion Poetry	£9.99
Rowland Bagnall	A Few Interiors	Carcanet Press	£9.99
Jay Bernard	Surge	Chatto & Windus	£10.00
Zoë Brigley	Hand & Skull	Bloodaxe Books	£9.95
Lucy Burnett	Tripping Over Clouds	Carcanet Press	£9.99
Kimberly Campanello	MOTHERBABYHOME	ZimZalla	£40.00
Neil Campbell	In the Gemini Café	KFS	£10.00
Niall Campbell	Noctuary	Bloodaxe Books	£9.95
Jen Campbell	The Girl Aquarium	Bloodaxe Books	£9.95
Vahni Capildeo	Skin Can Hold	Carcanet Press	£9.99
Chen Chen	When I Grow Up I Want to Be A List Of...	Bloodaxe Books	£9.95
Peter Dent	A Wind-Up Collider	Shearsman Books	£9.95
Joe Dunthorne	O Positive	Faber & Faber	£10.99
Inua Ellams	The Half God of Rainfall	Harper Collins	£10.00
U.A. Fanthorpe	Beginner's Luck	Bloodaxe Books	£9.95
Catherine Fisher	The Bramble King	Seren	£9.99
Miriam Gamble	What Planet	Bloodaxe Books	£9.95
Rebecca Goss	Girl	Carcanet Press	£9.99
John Greening	The Silence	Carcanet Press	£9.99
Vona Groarke	Double Negative	The Gallery Press	£10.50
Liam Guilar	A Presentment of Englishry	Shearsman Books	£9.95
Kendel Hippolyte	Wordplanting	Peepal Tree Press	£9.99
Tony Hoagland	Priest Turned Therapist Treats Fear of God	Bloodaxe Books	£9.95
Ranjit Hoskote	Jonahwhale	Arc Publications	£10.99
Ian Humphreys	Zebra	Nine Arches Press	£9.99
Helen Ivory	The Anatomical Venus	Bloodaxe Books	£9.95
Peter Jarvis	Land the Colour of Heat	Red Squirrel Press	£8.99
Math Jones	The Knotsman	Arachne Press	£9.99
Ilya Kaminsky	Deaf Republic	Faber & Faber	£10.99
Lisa Kelly	A Map Towards Fluency	Carcanet Press	£9.99
Nicholas Laughlin	Enemy Luck	Peepal Tree Press	£9.99
John Matthias	Acoustic Shadow	Shearsman Books	£10.95
Thomas McCarthy	Prophecy	Carcanet Press	£9.99
John McCullough	Reckless Paper Birds	Penned in the Margins	£9.99
Richard O'Brien	Dragons of the Prime: Poems about Dinosaurs	The Emma Press	£12.00
Michael O'Neill	Crash and Burn	Arc Publications	£9.99
Richard Osmond	Rock, Paper, Scissors	Picador	£10.99
Heather Phillipson	Whip-Hot & Grippy	Bloodaxe Books	£12.00
Frances Presley	Ada Unseen	Shearsman Books	£9.95
Sheenagh Pugh	Afternoons Go Nowhere	Seren	£9.99
Vidyan Ravinthiran	The Million-petalled Flower of Being Here	Bloodaxe Books	£9.95
Deryn Rees-Jones	Erato	Seren	£9.99
Various	The Laureate's Choice Anthology	Smith|Doorstop	£10.00
Patricia Smith	Incendiary Art	Bloodaxe Books	£12.00
Layli Long Soldier	Whereas	Picador	£10.99
Karen Solie	The Caiplie Caves	Picador	£10.99
Jon Thompson	Notebook of Last Things	Shearsman Books	£10.95
Adam Thorpe	Words From the Wall	Jonathan Cape	£10:00
Mark Waldron	Sweet, like Rinky-Dink	Bloodaxe Books	£9.95
Julia Webb	Threat	Nine Arches Press	£9.99
Hugo Williams	Lines Off	Faber & Faber	£14.99